The MARVELLOUS FUNAMBULIST of MIDDLE HARBOUR

and other Sydney firsts

{
Hilary Bell is a playwright,
That's how she spends most of her time.
She loves the strange tales of her city,
Especially making them rhyme.
}

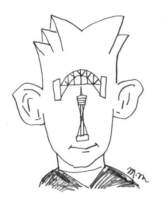

Matthew Martin draws pictures
and lives in Sydney. He even
looks like Sydney.

The MARVELLOUS FUNAMBULIST

of MIDDLE HARBOUR

and other Sydney firsts

Written by HILARY BELL

Illustrated by MATTHEW MARTIN

NEWSOUTH

To all the children of Sydney,
especially Ivy, Moss and Oscar

Contents

This is a story of Sydney
In order of who did what first:
The incidents, places and people,
All illustrated and versed.

Who first pulled a tooth using ether?
What started the first pistol fight?
When were the first Chinese tea rooms?
Where was the first traffic light?

Think you know all about cricket?
Or Billy Blue, in his top hat?
Or what lies beneath Town Hall Station:
Know anything about that?

Meet our genteel taxidermists.
Eat a revolving fondue.
Gaze at L'Estrange on his tightrope,
Or join him up there for the view.

First Sydneysiders

From sea to grasslands you could walk,
Trading bream for possum meat.
The tracks Eora people made
Are now called George and Oxford Street,
Still trading meat and fish today,
Still greeting friends along the way.

A place for special gatherings:
The swampland, now Centennial Park.
On the ridge we call Kings Cross,
A shellfish cook-up after dark
To dance and sing and eat a lot –
It's always been a party spot.

Up from Tamarama Beach,
A stingray hovers in the stone.
In a cave at La Perouse,
Handprints bright and white as bone,
And a basalt slippery-dip
Worn smooth before the first tall ship.

Though roads are hiding running streams,
And midden shells ground up for mortar,
Always was, will always be,
Sunrise, sandstone and saltwater.
Look – a rainbow lorikeet,
Home to roost on Oxford Street.

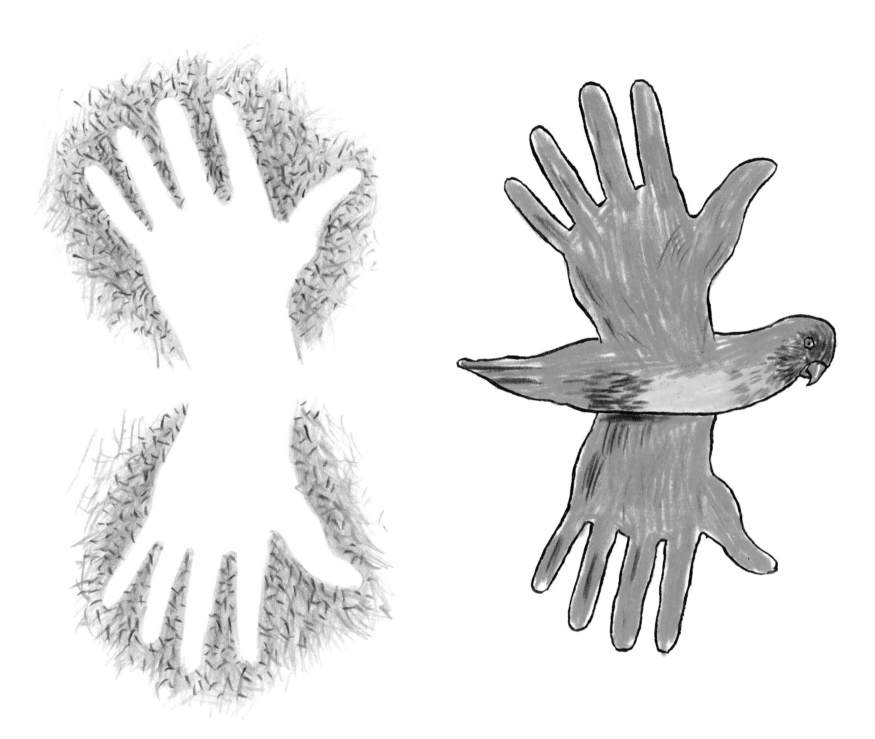

1788 First pistol duel, fought by First Fleet surgeons

Doctor Balmain and Doctor White
Didn't get on. Over dinner one night,
Each called the other names awfully cruel,
Until they agreed on one thing: a duel.

Right then and there, they stepped outside.
'If you'd draw blood', their poor host cried,
'Do it with lancets upon my sick mother.
Not, sirs, with pistols, and not from each other!'
Luckily, neither was good with a gun
Or instead of two doctors, there would've been none.

1792 First official European cemetery

Here they buried Sydney's dead
The celebrated, and unknown.
Soldiers, convicts, businessmen
Mouldered under marble stone
Till there was room for nothing more,
Not a single finger bone.

It soon fell into disrepair,
The grass grew high, the headstones fell.
At night, the living haunted it –
The lowest sort of ne'er-do-well.
While daytime saw it overrun
By goats and pigs.
           And oh,
                the smell!

The stench arising from the ground
Was foul enough in cold July,
But sniff it in the summer heat –
The passers-by would rather die!
Conveniently, coffin thieves
Left open graves just standing by.

In due course they built Town Hall,
Replacing tombs with pipes and drains.
Underneath came Town Hall Station:
That dislodged some more remains.
Ponder this on Platform Six
When you next are changing trains.

1830 (ish) First ferryman to charge a fare: Billy Blue

Billy Blue is known to all and sundry.
His old top hat and coloured tatters suit him.
He strolls along the lane
A-twirling of his cane,
Demanding ladies curtsey, men salute him.

Transported for the crime of stealing sugar,
He's made a living fruit-and-veggie growing.
The weary and the merry
He rows home on his ferry –
Or takes a nap, and lets them do the rowing.

1847 First use of ether by a dental surgeon

Belisario held the inhaler
And presto, his patient was dreaming.
Did he guess, when apprenticed,
He'd be our first dentist
To pull out a tooth with no screaming?

They raged in the medical journals,
They called it a 'dangerous fad'.
While their forceps and screws
Are yesterday's news,
Anaesthetic remains. And I'm glad.

1868 First cricket team to leave Sydney for an overseas tour

With much excited chatter,
They board the *Parramatta*,
Conversation turned towards
Glory, victory, and Lord's.
Through Sydney Heads, full-steam:
Our all-black cricket team.

Charley Dumas and Jim Crow,
Sundown, Red Cap, Mosquito,
Bullocky and Dick-a-Dick
(One can catch and one moves quick),
Johnny Mullagh, Tiger, Peter
(Hit that ball a kilometre!),
Johnny Cuzens and King Cole.
But to see the fastest bowl,
You could search and not find any
Better man than Tom Twopenny.

At Lord's, they're a sensation.
Jim gives a demonstration
Spear throwing. How the punters quake!
He kills a squirrel by mistake.
The Londoners are smitten.
Now for the rest of Britain.

Testing Aussie grit and sinews,
On the gruelling tour continues.
Tom drives everyone insane
By nearly missing every train.
Matches lost and matches won,
All even by the time they're done.
Finally, they brave the foam
And proudly point the prow for home.

They're stars in Cricket Heaven,
Our all-black First Eleven.

1872 First mother-and-daughter taxidermy business: Tost & Rohu

Ada and her mother Jane
Own a shop. Among its features:
Native reptiles, birds and beasts,
Lifeless stuffed and mounted creatures.

They work with wire, wood-wool, wax,
Paint and plaster, small glass eyes,
Mixing powdered chalk and arsenic,
Stitching skin before it dries.

Here's a staring bandicoot;
Starfish, pickled good and proper;
Here's a possum turning green
(Someone's using too much copper).

Ada and her mother Jane
Win medals and museum sales.
People travel far to see
The queerest shop in New South Wales.

1877 First crossing of Middle Harbour by tightrope: Henri L'Estrange

A poster, a tent and a tightrope
Were rigged up in Sydney's Domain.
Curious folk
Peered inside: there, a bloke
Waved from his chair ...
Forty feet in the air!
Then he tootled along
On his bike, in full song,
And he walked forth and back
With his head in a sack.
That funambulist charmer
Then walked it in armour;
They laughed as they looked,
For he stopped – and he cooked.
This up on a rope, did I mention?
Some said he was after attention,
Some said it was glory and gain.
Some thought he was mad as a herring.
In fact, he was merely preparing ...

Soon there were ads in the papers,
Soon there were tickets for sale.
Construction began
On his daredevil plan:
Held with many a tether
Against windy weather
From cliff to far slope
Was a very long rope,
'Strung across Middle Harbour!'
Said lawyer to barber,
'With guy rope and anchor!'
Said shopgirl to banker,
'Incredibly high,
If he falls in, he'll die!'
Ten thousand or more
Flocked the harbour and shore
And they wondered if now life would change,
As they waited for Henri L'Estrange.
He appeared (just a little bit pale)
In a tunic, a turban and cape.
And he smiled at the crowd: no escape.

He took one step
then one more
left behind
the shrinking shore
reached the centre
breathed aloud
waved his hanky
for the crowd
walked three-quarters of the rope
took a pocket telescope
then surveyed the gaping throng,
thinking, 'Lord, I hope it's strong'.
Lay down,
stood,
one final bend
...
walked briskly to the other end.

Up went a cheer from the masses,
Up struck the three brass bands.
Rowboats and steamers
Blew whistles, threw streamers.
'He Walks Across Water!'
Proclaimed a reporter.
To see at close range
This Henri L'Estrange
They crowded the bay,
It was quite a melee
(The banker and barber
Fell into the harbour).
He spawned imitators
But none were as great as
L'Estrange. Sydney owes him a mention.
Did he hazard his life for attention?
The applause of untold pairs of hands?
Perhaps it was only because
Up there, nothing was high as he was.

1882 First grand building on fire: the Garden Palace

Six o'clock, and Sydney slept.
Someone crept across the lawn.
A spark became a lick of flame,
Smoking through a blood-red dawn.

Fiery fingers fondled timber,
Billowed out like giant sails,
A wild inferno roared. They were no
Match, those horse-drawn trucks with pails.

A grand caprice of gilded tower,
Lacy turret, colonnade,
A giant dome – St Peter's, Rome
Beat it only by a shade.
Bigger than two football fields,
Taller than the great Town Hall,
The city's pride. Now, horrified,
Bystanders watched it burst and fall.

Hours ago in all its glory
Here the Garden Palace stood.
By nine o'clock, the awful shock
Of twisted metal, blackened wood.

Why burn such a wonder down?
They found no culprit and no clues.
Perhaps elite Macquarie Street
Simply missed its harbour views.

1891 First Chinese tea rooms: Quong Tart's

Quong Tart's Tea Rooms on King Street
Serve up every kind of treat:
Chinese tea and English meals
Lapsang souchong, jellied eels,
With marble ponds and mirrored walls,
Reading rooms and banquet halls.

Besides pu-erh and pickled beef,
Quong Tart's Tea Rooms bring relief:
Sydney has its public loos ...
Which women aren't allowed to use.
Quong introduces 'powder rooms':
Women flock and business booms!

It soon becomes a social hub:
The Sydney Ladies' Bicycle Club
Forms there, proudly captained by
Sarah Maddock (blind, one eye).
Louisa Lawson likes a scone:
The Dawn Club's in the front salon.
Suffragettes, led by Rose Scott
Rise up over cup and pot.

Tea and politics:
Who says they don't mix?

1915 First surfer-girl, Isabel Letham, rides with Duke Kahanamoku

He wowed the crowd at Dee Why
By paddling out a mile,
Then leapt up, with a smile,
Shot surf, Hawaiian-style.
It isn't hard to see why
They cheered and yelled for more.
Young Isabel was small and light.
'Come here', he said, 'and hold on tight'.

Fifteen years old and knee-high,
The tomboy jumped aboard.
She heard the crowd applaud.
Then, before her soared
A wave: enormous, tree-high!
The girl was petrified.
'Up you stand now!' laughed the Duke.
She thought that she would surely puke.

They sailed right over Dee Why.
Her terror fell away.
They flew across the bay
Like seagulls through the spray ...

Until they toppled backwards.
WIPEOUT!
                But Isabel,
Who'd skimmed the water like a comet
Holds the title: Our First Grommet.

31

1933 First traffic light

The first traffic light was on Market and Kent.
Cars stopped on red, and on green off they went.
Before they installed it, imagine the havoc!
'Thank God', sighed the copper directing the traffic,
Far fewer bingles and prangs now, he reckoned.
Still, took them four years till they built him a second.

1960 First Opera House concert (construction site): Paul Robeson

Some have never heard of him,
Some don't care for singing, neither.
But they gladly down their tools –
Anything to take a breather.

Here he comes: a tall black man,
Flower in his buttonhole,
Cups his ear. His first deep note
Rolls like thunder through the soul.

He stands there in the open air
Among the pipes and wet concrete,
Cables, girders, scaffolding,
His velvet rumble warm and sweet.

Seagulls wheeling overhead
Blink back tears, their eyes a-glisten.
Distant ferries mute their horns,
A buzzing fly stops by to listen.

Through the crowd of burly blokes
'Ol' Man River' laps its way.
'What you're building here', he says,
'Is going to make you proud one day'.

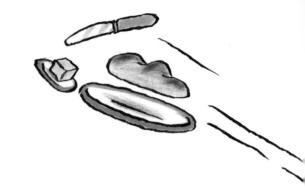

1968 First revolving restaurant: the Summit

Vol-au-vents
Cheese fondue
Meatloaf
Devilled eggs for two
Wiener schnitzel
Prawn cocktails
If you're feeling daring,
Snails.

Gradually, round we go,
Have no fear, it's very slow.
There's the Harbour Bridge below,
Everything looks weeny.
Waiter! One martini.

Round and round Australia Square,
You'll see everything up there.
Here comes your aperitif,
Toast Hyde Park, it's in full leaf.
Look at all the pigeon poop
On the statues. – Here's your soup.
Now we're passing Watsons Bay,
Waiter please, a clean ashtray.
Malabar before the mains;
On a clear day, Emu Plains.
The Spit at forty-five degrees.
Ooh, dessert flambé? Yes please.

Wish it didn't move so slow.
Here's the dance floor: go man go!
There's a ferry, miles below.
What's wrong, darling? Dizzy?
Waiter! Jeez, where is 'e?

1979 First dancing-horse theme park: El Caballo Blanco

El Caballo Blanco:
You feel like you're living in Spain.
Well, less Andalucía,
More Minto, near the train.
Some come here for the go-karts
Some for the waterslides
Some for the souvenir shop
Some for the carriage rides.
But what's the main attraction?
What most of all appeals?
Think glittering mantillas,
Think sequins, Cuban heels,
The frowning flamencistas,
The men in gold medallions,
And brightest of the highlights:
The Spanish dancing stallions!
They bow a feathered forelock,
They shake a plaited mane,
They lift their hooves as one …
Perhaps it *is* a bit like Spain.

2000 First Sydney Olympic Games

It flickers to life from the rays of the sun,
The flame lights the torch, and the relay's begun.
From Athens it travels to Guam, and then Tonga;
A Wellington haka makes it burn stronger.
An aeroplane carries it into the blue,
And reaches Australia. First: Uluru.
Then ...

On foot and on bicycle, camel and train
It travels the coast and the Nullarbor Plain,
Through water to cross the Great Barrier Reef
(And doesn't go out, which is quite a relief).
All the way south to the Blowhole, Kiama,
Cheered on by one hundred bikies – the clamour!
When half of the world and a country's been spanned,
The torch comes to rest in our own Cathy's hand.

The cauldron is lit ... but it doesn't ascend.
Such an odyssey, such an embarrassing end!
Scrambling technicians press buttons, and sweat.
Water keeps falling. Poor Cathy's quite wet.
The world holds its breath – and then gives a great sigh
As up goes the cauldron aflame, to the sky.

2013 First rainbow crossing

One glorious morning the city awoke
To find on the road at Taylor Square
A magical rainbow, a beautiful joke,
In place of the crossing that once was there.

From out of the blue, it brightened the day,
Sunshine or rain, its colours shone.
But the end of the rainbow was not far away:
The city woke up, and it was gone.

All of us missed that happy cross-walk.
And then, in a lane, we found red and blue,
Yellow and indigo stripes, in chalk.
Soon everyone else was drawing, too.

Rainbows appeared from Box Hill to Bondi,
Then Launceston, Broome, Shanghai, New York,
All over the planet! So keep a sharp eye,
And if you don't see one, pick up some chalk.

The Firsts: second helpings

Here are some more facts about the stories in this book.

First Sydneysiders

The place we now call Sydney was first home to the Gadigal, one of about 29 clans who make up the Eora Nation. The Dharug occupy the land from Parramatta to the Blue Mountains. The north is home to the Gayamaygal, and the south to the Dharawal. The first Sydneysiders arrived somewhere between 50 000 and 125 000 years ago. The various clans were distinguished by their languages, body decorations, tools and weapons, and songs and dances. Coastal men had their right incisor tooth knocked out in their initiation ceremony. It happened that Governor Phillip was missing the same tooth, which caused great excitement when the Eora first saw him.

1788 • First pistol duel, fought by First Fleet surgeons

William Balmain was surgeon John White's assistant. Their host at the duelling dinner was Governor Phillip, and the dinner was held to celebrate the Prince of Wales' birthday. Two years later, William Balmain would remove a spear from Governor Phillip's shoulder. The spear was payback from the Garigal clan for the Europeans' kidnapping of Bennelong ... but that's another story.

1792 • First official European cemetery

Europeans and Aboriginal people were buried in the first cemetery, known as the Old Sydney Burial Ground, located where Sydney Town Hall now stands. Look for a tiny plaque above an alcove outside the train station that is dedicated to the people of the First Fleet. The burial grounds had to be moved further away as the settlement grew. After the Town Hall spot the cemetery was moved to Devonshire Street (now Central Station).

1830 (ish) • First ferryman to charge a fare: Billy Blue

Billy Blue was of African descent, born in New York and working in London when he was convicted of stealing sugar (to make chocolate!). Those who didn't salute him when he demanded it copped a heap of fruity abuse. He was perhaps Sydney's first celebrity, and a favourite of Governor and Lady Macquarie, who built him a hut on what is now Blues Point. His nickname was The Commodore, and today The Commodore Hotel stands where the Billy Blue Inn once stood on Blues Point Road.

1847 • First use of ether by a dental surgeon

It was not only dentists who were experimenting with ether. Along with Mr John Belisario, 'Surgeon-Dentist', Sydney Hospital's first surgeon, Dr Charles Nathan, was an ether pioneer. He made the papers in 1868. At a picnic in Clontarf, an Irishman made an attempt on the life of Prince Alfred, the Duke of Edinburgh, who was visiting Australia. Dr Nathan was among the surgeons who managed to extract the bullet (First Bullet Extracted From a Prince: another Sydney 'first'). The prince was commemorated in the naming of the Royal Prince Alfred Hospital in Camperdown.

1868 • First cricket team to leave Sydney for an overseas tour

Throughout the English tour, Tom Twopenny (Murrumgunarriman) was famous for arriving at train stations at the last minute. The team's managers found the players' tribal names too difficult to pronounce, so gave them English nicknames. Here are their nicknames and traditional names (spellings vary). There may also have been other players who travelled with the team.

Johnny Mullagh – Unaarrimin
Bullocky – Bullchanach
Sundown – Ballrinjarrimin
Dick-a-Dick – Jungumjenanuke
Johnny Cuzens – Yellanach
King Cole – Bripumyarrumin
Tommy Red Cap – Brimbunyah
Tom Twopenny – Murrumgunarriman
Charley Dumas – Pripumuarraman
Jimmy Mosquito – Grongarrong
Tiger – Bonnibarngeet
Peter – Arrahmunyarrimun
Jim Crow – Lyterjebillijun

1872 • First mother-and-daughter taxidermy business: Tost & Rohu

Although taxidermy was a leisure activity for middle-class women in the nineteenth century, Jane Tost and Ada Rohu were hard workers. Jane was the Australian Museum's first female employee. As well as carved emu eggs, wax fruit, feather flowers and human skulls, their shop displayed 'an electrical machine, a working model circus, mechanical figures and a galvanic battery', and live snakes – including a python that was 4 metres long!

1877 • First crossing of Middle Harbour by tightrope: Henri L'Estrange

After this feat, Henri L'Estrange moved on to aeronautical experiments. In 1880 his hot air balloon drifted over the Garden Palace and towards the Pacific Ocean. Trying to land before being swept out to sea, he got tangled in trees and brambles. His next attempt saw him stuck on a rooftop in Woolloomooloo, where the balloon's gas caused an explosion. Death-defying feats were all the rage at the time. In 1890 Val Van Tassel made the news as the first female parachutist, her hot air balloon floating over Bondi and along the coast until she jumped out and landed in a mud hole in Coogee.

1882 • First grand building on fire: the Garden Palace

A rush job for the Sydney International Exhibition of 1879 – men worked around the clock for 8 months, including by arc light at night – the Garden Palace was made almost entirely of timber: its destruction only took 40 minutes. Although no one has ever found out who or what caused the fire, some people believe it was an electrical fault, while others think the fire was deliberately lit, perhaps to destroy documents stored there – including records that linked respectable people to their convict ancestors. The Garden Palace gates still stand in the Royal Botanic Gardens. Two more Sydney firsts: the Palace boasted the first hydraulic lift and the first steam tramline.

1891 • First Chinese tea rooms: Quong Tart's

Mei Quong Tart arrived on the New South Wales goldfields as a child, and was adopted by a Scottish couple, the Simpsons. He grew up with a Scottish accent, and a passion for the poet Robert Burns, bagpipes and wearing a kilt. As well as the Loong Shan Tea Giyse on King Street, he had tea rooms in the Queen Victoria Market Building, Moore Park Zoo and in Haymarket's theatre district. *The Dawn* was a feminist newspaper created by Louisa Lawson, mother of the writer Henry Lawson.

1915 • First surfer-girl, Isabel Letham, rides with Duke Kahanamoku

The wave that Isabel and Duke rode may not have been all that spectacular, and it does seem to have ended with both of them being wiped out. Sydney's first male surfer was Tommy Walker, who was admired surfing at Manly in 1912 on a board he'd boug' t in Hawaii for $2. Bodysurfing in Sydney had been around for much longer: in 1788, British officer Watkin Tench observed two Gadigal women bodysurfing on bark in Sydney Harbour.

1933 • First traffic light

Sydney started looking for ways to manage its traffic from the days of drays and herds of cattle, demanding a toll from travellers along the Sydney–Parramatta Road that opened in 1811. Congestion got worse through that century, until by 1888 there were 400 horse-drawn omnibuses, 1000 horse-drawn cabs and 500 delivery vans in Sydney. Along with 1933's single traffic light came 100 or so pedestrian crossings. In 1945, soldiers who had returned from World War II with disabilities were put on duty as parking officers, with the first parking meters appearing in 1956.

1960 • First Opera House concert (construction site): Paul Robeson

Paul Robeson was an American singer and actor. He was hugely popular with audiences in the 1930s and 1940s, but not so popular with the US Government, which did not like him speaking out about human rights, racial discrimination and the rights of workers. His views meant he was banned from performing in venues in America for many years. When he visited Australia to perform, he gave several impromptu performances for wharfies and builders.

1968 • First revolving restaurant: the Summit
The revolving restaurant was at the top of Australia Square, on the forty-seventh floor. The 1960s was also the era of floating restaurants (Flanagan's Afloat in Rose Bay, which later became the Imperial Peking) and theatre restaurants (Dirty Dick's is still going in Rydalmere). It's interesting to note the way dishes go in and out of fashion. Chilled celery log, anyone?

1979 • First dancing-horse theme park: El Caballo Blanco
The theme park is long gone, but the descendants of those dancing horses are still there, living wild in the outer suburbs of Sydney. Another favourite theme park to open in the 1970s was Old Sydney Town, with its thatching demonstrations, butter churning and three o'clock matinee floggings. But Sydney's first amusement park, in 1906, was Tamarama's Wonderland City, complete with ice-skating rink, rides, a Japanese tea room and an elephant.

2000 • First Sydney Olympic Games
The story didn't end there. Cathy Freeman left her distinctive white bodysuit, which got soaking wet during the technical delay, in the changing room, and it disappeared. Fifteen years later it was mysteriously returned. Was it the original suit? Yes, the designer could prove it: she had been up late sewing the night before the event, and had absent-mindedly sewn the Olympic rings on upside down.

2013 • First rainbow crossing
Rainbow crossings sprang up all over Sydney after the first one in Taylor Square. The children and parents of Summer Hill chalked their own rainbow, only to have it removed by Ashfield Council. They chalked it again, and it was once again removed. Finally people power won, and Summer Hill now has a permanent rainbow in Lackey Street Plaza. Chalk rainbows continue to appear around the world as a symbol of solidarity and love.

A NewSouth book

Published by
NewSouth Publishing
University of New South Wales Press Ltd
University of New South Wales
Sydney NSW 2052
AUSTRALIA
newsouthpublishing.com

First published 2015

10 9 8 7 6 5 4 3 2 1

National Library of Australia Cataloguing-in-Publication entry

Creator: Bell, Hilary, author.
Title: The Marvellous Funambulist of Middle Harbour and Other Sydney Firsts / Hilary Bell;
    Matthew Martin.
ISBN: 9781742234403 (hardback)
Target audience: For primary school age.
Subjects: Stories in rhyme.
    Sydney (NSW) – Miscellanea.
    Sydney (NSW) – History – Juvenile literature.
Other creators/contributors: Martin, Matthew, illustrator.
Dewey Number: 994.41

Design Josephine Pajor-Markus
Cover design Design by Committee
Printer 1010